Drawing Spiders
Volume 2
How to Draw Spiders
For the Beginner

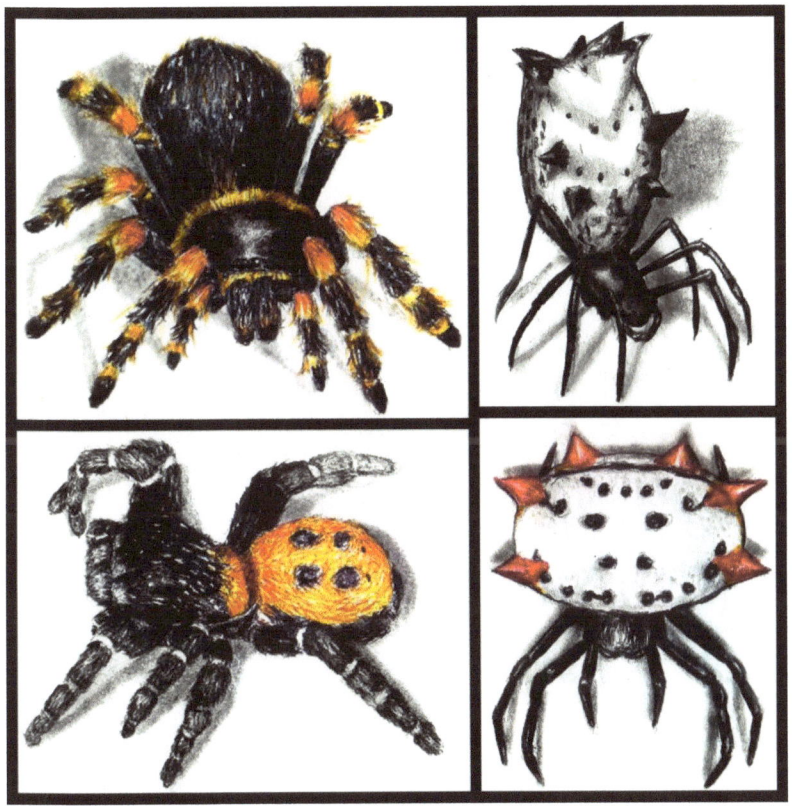

Adrian Sanqui
And
John Davidson

Learn to Draw Series
Mendon Cottage Books
JD- Biz Publishing

Learn How to Draw Books for the Absolute Beginner

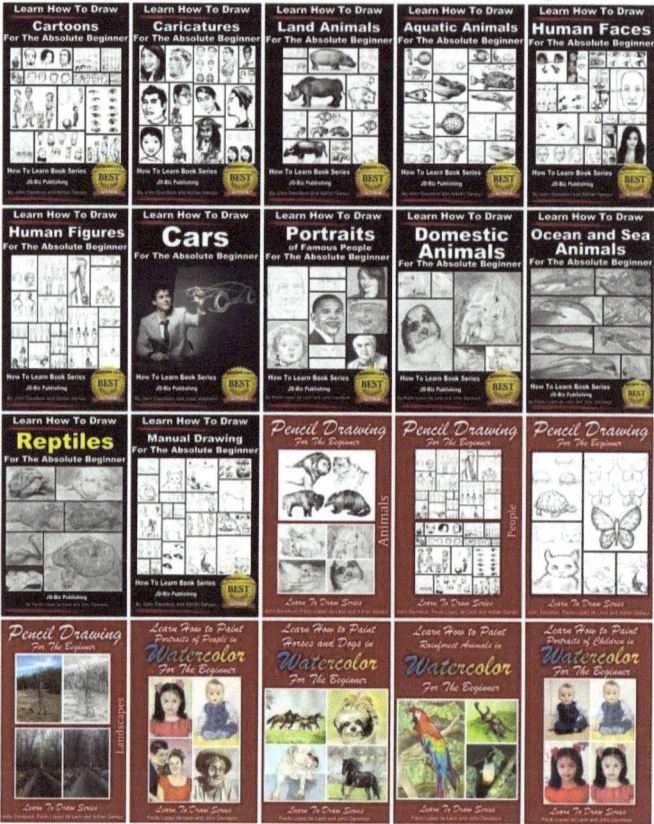

TABLE OF CONTENTS

Drawing tools

Pencils

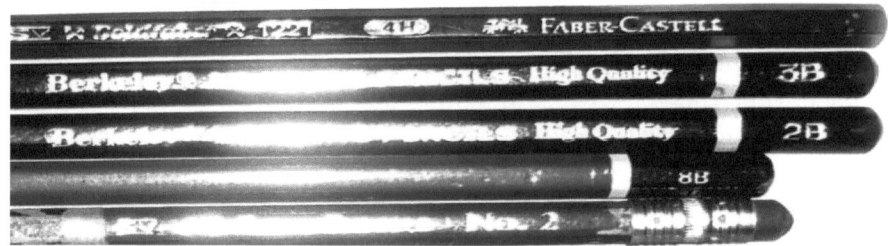

The most important tool you need to be able to enhance your drawing skills is a medium that can be corrected if you made some sloppy line strokes. Knowing and using more than just one type of pencil is a big help and it is better if you have pencils of different grades so you can easily produce the kind of lightness or darkness you want to make. The 'H' engraved near the pencil's tip (side of eraser) stands for "hardness" and it ranges from 2H to 9H. A pencil with only an "H" mark and doesn't have a number means 1H. The most common type (the one available anywhere) of pencil that does not indicate its grade mark is usually a 2H pencil. The "B" marking of pencils stand for "blackness", this means that they can easily produce darker line marks and are softer than H pencils. It ranges from HB (hard and dark) to 9B (very soft and very dark), so when it comes to B pencils, the higher the number is; the softer and darker it becomes. Different brands have different softness, hardness and blackness levels, so if you are going to use a certain brand for the first time, you should try them out first before applying it on your main drawing.

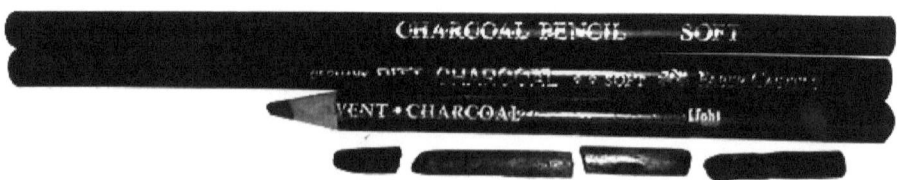

Charcoal pencils also come in different grades. The generic grades of soft, medium and hard are available in different brands. Charcoal pencils are a bit messy to work with; even the 'hard' grade charcoal pencil is still relatively softer compared to those with 4B to 6B grade pencils. It is most advisable for drawings that would require a lot of smeared shading for a smoother and wider portrayal of gradation.

Mechanical

pencil

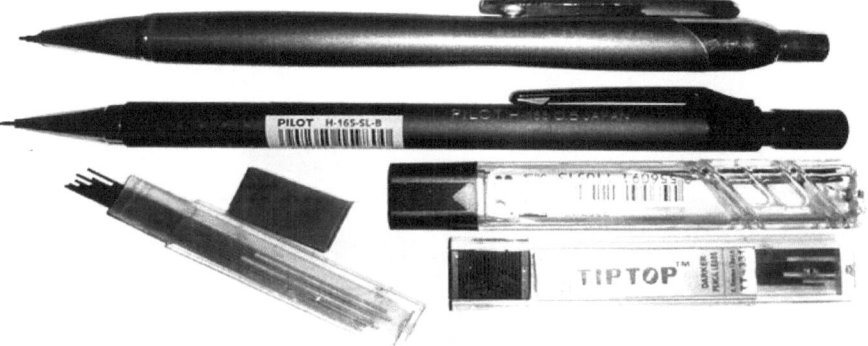

A mechanical pencil has a consistent wick or point which makes it easier for you to maintain the thickness of the line marks you produce. Mechanical pencils are good for small and subtle detailing that requires very thin lines, instead of sharpening your pencil several times just to have a thin and constant fine point that you need. Different grades of lead or graphite is also available for refilling your mechanical pencil, just make sure that the size of the point your pencil has is also the same as the pencil leads you refill it with. They come in several sizes and style, but what really matters is it does what it's supposed to.

Sharpener

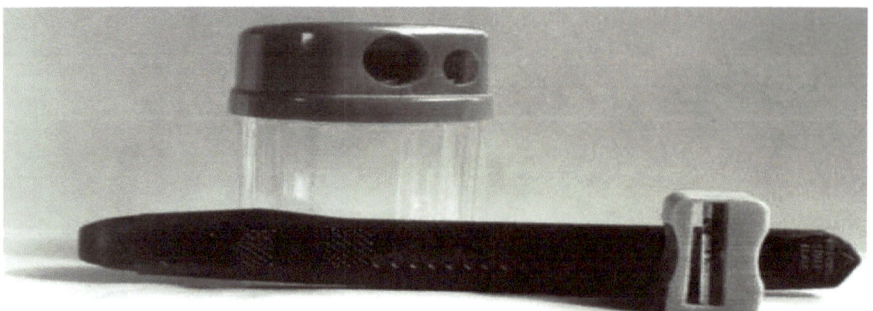

A regular sharpener is quite dependable if you are using H and low B pencils, but if you are going to use it to sharpen a pencil with very soft graphite cores then it may keep on breaking, most especially if you will use it for a charcoal lead pencil. A good substitute for regular sharpeners is a cutter, so you can easily control the pressure that should just be enough to expose the core and achieve a fine point. Cutters are often used if you want a "chisel" point pencil that is very helpful for thick and thin linings.

Erasers

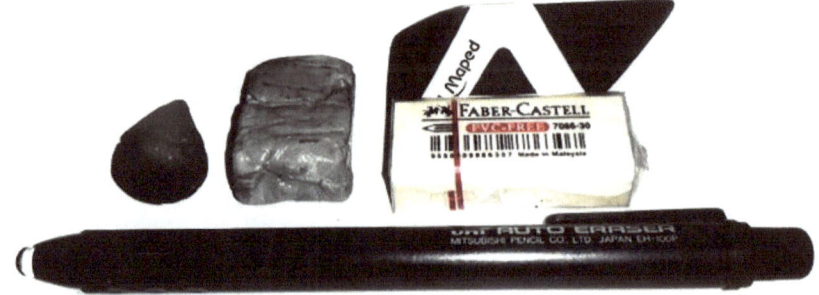

Pencils are no good if you don't have a good quality eraser, having an eraser is essential if you are going to use a pencil for drawing. Choose a rubber eraser that is soft and not the ones that leave a faint color or worst is a scratch on the paper. Don't leave your eraser lying around on the table or just anywhere, keep it on a pencil case or anything that can protect it from being exposed on air for too long because some erasers (cheaper ones) harden when it's left lying around because it will dry out and harden.

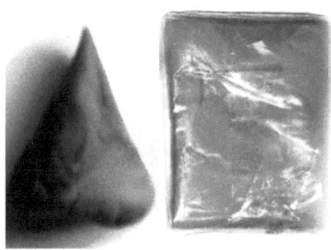

A kneadable eraser is very helpful for making highlights and reaching hardly accessible areas such as the gloss on the eyes or light portions of fingernails and such. It usually looks like a gray slab or a small bar of clay that can be molded or deformed to any shape you desire. It doesn't rub off the marking like usual erasers, but instead, it lifts off the graphite from the paper, like absorbing it. Instead of rubbing the eraser with a certain pressure to remove a marking, carefully dab on the portions you want to erase or to simply decrease the applied graphite or charcoal until you recover the brightness (whiteness of the paper) you want. Kneaded erasers can still be useful as long as they aren't already too dirty or dry. Keep it in a concealed container to lengthen its usefulness, because just like how good it is for absorbing graphite, it would also easily catch dust.

Smudge
sticks

A smudge stick is used for smearing the shades on the portions that are hard to access. Some artists dull down the other tip so it can be used for distributing the shades on the big areas. To avoid ruining the smudge stick, use a sand paper to make a blunter tip or to make it even pointier. Smudge sticks or blending stumps comes in different sizes, choose what best fits your needs and it will be a big help for blending gradations. Smudge sticks are cheap and are available on art stores. Common smudge sticks are just rolled and compressed hard papers, so try not to get it wet.

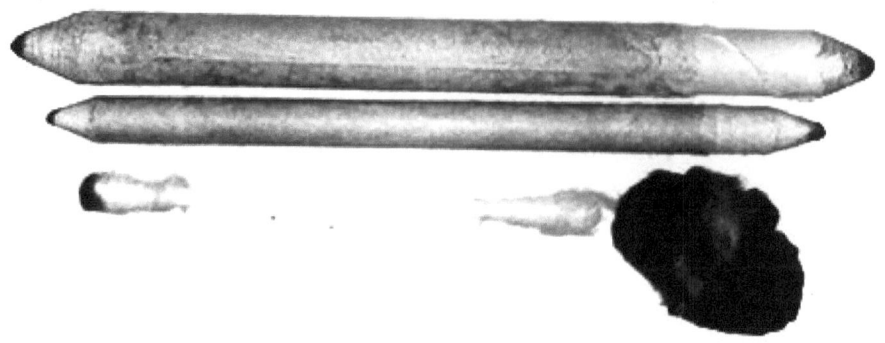

Keep those used up smudge sticks even if it's already in a rugged state (dirty or worn out), you never know when it might get handy. Dirty smudge sticks are useful for producing faint shades, and those with torn up tips can make textures that you might find useful.

If ever you cannot find a smudge stick available (although, I doubt this would be a problem if you have art stores near you, and if not, you can just order online. It is quite cheap) you can just make a tortillion for a temporary smudging tool (some artists actually prefer this one instead of smudge sticks). Use a thick piece of paper (like those on sketch pads, preferably the ones for watercolor drawings. Do not use thin and shiny papers). Fold it on one side and roll it up to create a cone, with the folded side at the tip.

Coloring materials

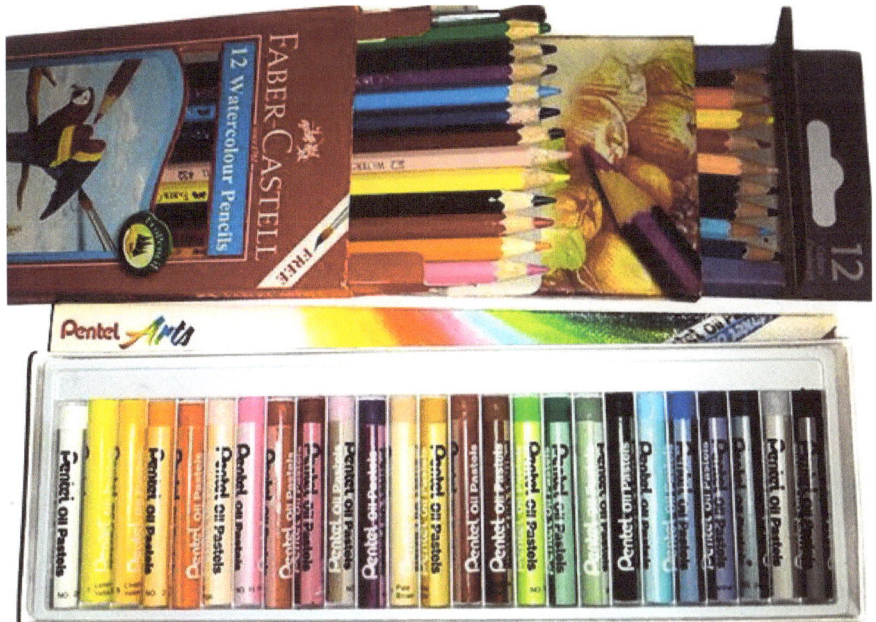

If you are planning to color your drawing, choose a coloring tool that best fits your needs.

Oil pastels are good for blending and synchronizing different colors together. It might get messy on your first trials (if you don't want to get messy, just place a clean piece of paper for your palm rest, to avoid rubbing your palm against the colored portions of your drawing) but you'll get the hang of it as you use it more often. Oil pastels are good for beginners as a practicing tool for smearing different color values.

Color pencils are the next best thing for filling your drawing with colored hatches (linear shading), or even coloring via scribbling. This coloring tool is best for small-sized illustrations. Although, the peak of the tone values that a common color pencil set can produce are far weaker than the oil pastel's, and it cannot be smeared (but there are available color pencils which can produce strong color tones just like oil pastel's or even acrylic's, but they are quite pricy; like the prisma color pencils). This coloring tool is also a good practicing medium for beginners, and my personal favorite for quick colored sketches or even for illustrations with fairly detailed line work.

Parts of a Spider

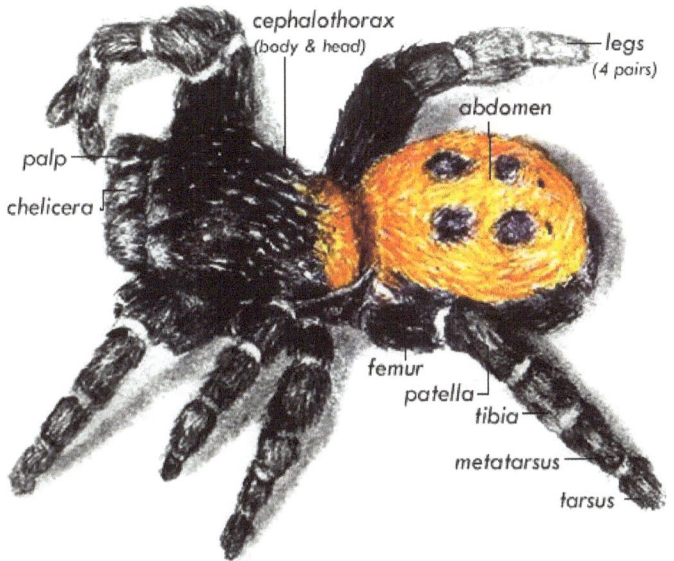

cephalothorax
(body & head)

legs
(4 pairs)

abdomen

palp

chelicera

femur
patella
tibia
metatarsus
tarsus

A spider's body structure is divided into two major parts. The upper portion is the cephalothorax (also called prosoma); this includes the spider's head and the thorax. The carapace covers the dorsal side (backside) of the upper body. At the center of the front edge of the head are the palps (the fangs/chelicera are at the lower center of the palps and are usually unnoticable to many species of spiders), and right above the palps are the eyes (number of eyes may differ, either eight or six depending on the breed). The main pair of eyes at the center is usually bigger compared to others. A minor dent/ dimple at the center of the carapace is the fovea, this is usually where the markings of the carapace start (especially on several kinds of tarantulas).

The lower part of the spider's body is its abdomen which is also called opisthosoma. The abdomen is always bigger in size and mass. At the center of the abdomen is the cardiac mark, it may or may not be visible to the other spiders especially those with uniquely shaped abdomens. At the lower edge of the abdomen where the silk comes out is called the spinner, this is barely seen (hidden most of the time) on a spider's dorsal view. Spiders have four pairs of legs (8 in total), and all are connected ventrally (underside) to the prosoma. A spider's leg is composed of 7 segments; the coxa which is connected to the base/upper body, followed by the trochanter which connects the coxa to the femur (the thickest and is usually the longest segment of the leg), then the joint which is the spider's knee called patella, followed by the tibia, metatarsus, and the tarsus which is the leg's tip.

Gasteracantha Cancriformis

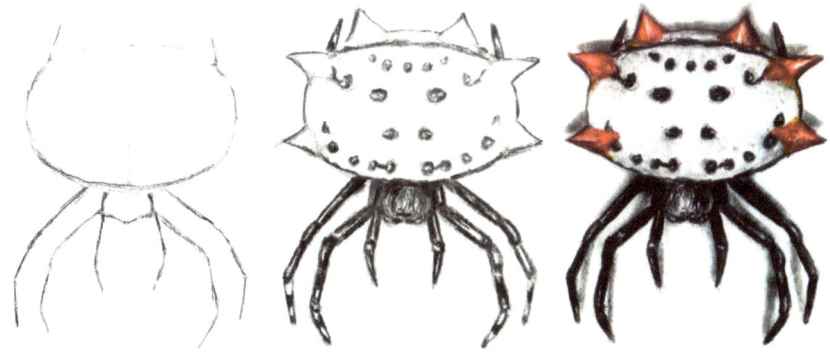

This orbweaving spider comes in many different names; spiny orbweaver spider, spiny bellied orbweaver, crab-like orbweaver, jewel box spider, the star spider, etc. These names are made to describe its wide and spiky oval-shaped abdomen which separates it from the others of the same species. It also referred as the smiley-face (the yellow-colored variety) due to the manner of dot formations (dorsal view) on its abdomen/opisthosoma.

The body of a gastheracantha cancriformis is generally black, excluding the oval abdomen, having few white short hairs. The limbs are typical to orbweaving spiders', and some containing faint stripes of brown or copper tone along the metatarsus (hind legs). The unique form of the abdomen is basically oval-shaped, containing 6 short thick spines (three pairs) along the edges of the dorsal side pointing outward, with two pairs on both sides and one pair on top-end. The dorsal color of the abdomen could be yellow or dirty white. Those with white upper sides could have red or black spines, while those with yellow only have black spines. The abdomen always contains black spots, which is always in the same linear formation.

There are 19 irregular spots that are uniformly arranged to 4 rows in a diagonal position on the dorsal side (head at the bottom). The first row are curved with the oval surface contour of the abdomen, containing five small dots, and the next row has 4 bigger dots at the mid-center of the abdomen, followed by a row with slightly smaller dots having two, and the row (also curved) at the near-bottom of the abdomen contains 8 small dots. The small black dots on the near edges of the abdomen are sometimes linked together, but the number of bigger dots at the center is always the same.

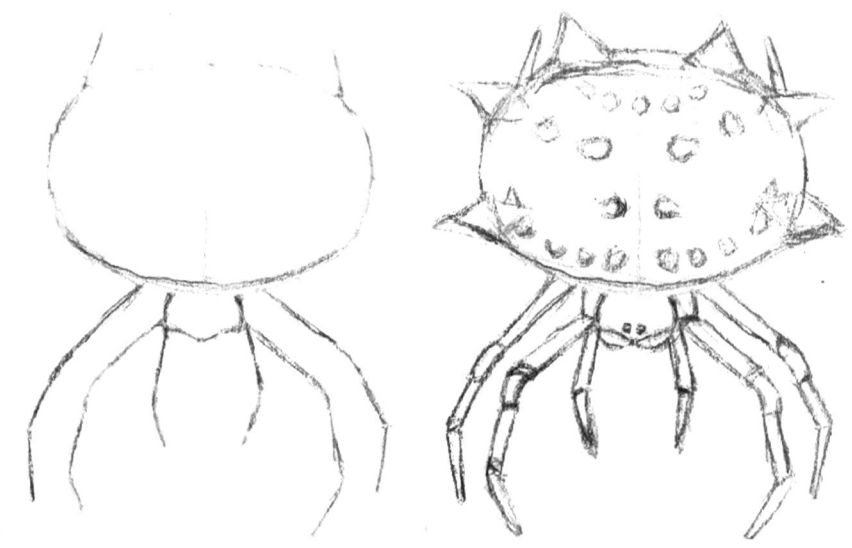

- Start with the simplest form.

The oval abdomen of a gasteracantha cancriformis is quite thick (like of crab's); in ventral view, the lower half of the upper body/cephalothorax is usually hidden/overlapped and only the head can be seen.

Start establishing the shape with the abdomen. Find the center of the oval and mark it with a vertical line, and then draw the head right below the reference line. Establish the length of the exposed limbs using simple stick lines.

- Add the details of the abdomen.

Place the spines of the abdomen properly, there should be four thick spikes at the side edges of the oval and then another pair on top it. Use the reference line to equally level the dot marks of the abdomen. Start with the four dots at the center, with the first pair having more gap in between. Add two more dots right next to first pair of dots on a slightly higher level (to form a row of arc). Draw five smaller dots near the edge of the oval's upper area (also in an arc form) with the third dot at the center of the reference line. And at the lower edge, draw eight smaller dots with the fourth and fifth aligning with the pair of dots above it.

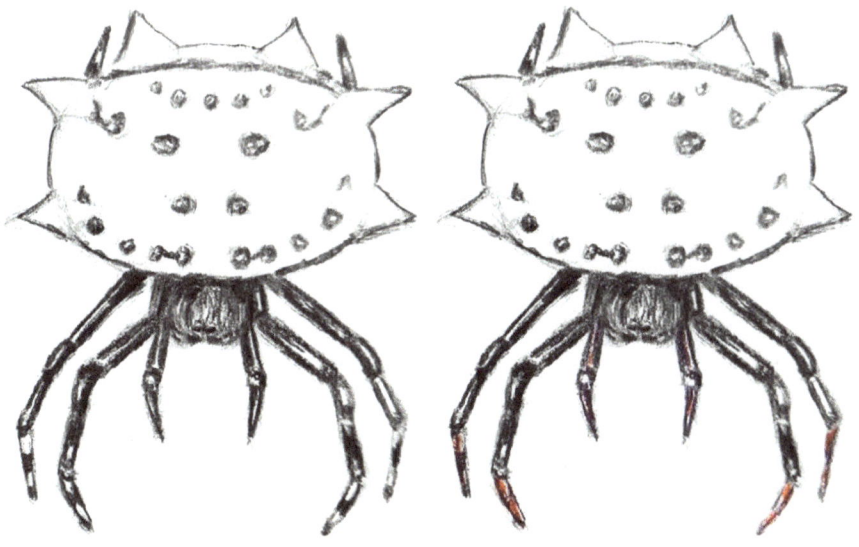

- Shade the areas that should be dark.

Once all the details of the abdomen are properly placed, erase the reference line and shade these dot marks. Apply a darker and thicker shade at the top and bottom sides of each dots. Thicken the margining outline of the abdomen's top and bottom outline; these outlining edges are black (in contrast to the bright color of the abdomen). Apply some shade to the body as well; shade the near edges of the limbs to effectively convey their cylindrical contour shape. Use linear shading/hatches for the head to portray its partly hairy texture.

- Apply the brown tone of the limbs.

Color the last segment of the legs (from metatarsus to tarsus) with light/copper brown. And also apply a brown color to the palps.

- Smear the shades.

Carefully smudges the shades of the limbs to produce a gray tone at the middle areas that should appear darker (than the brightest portions). Leave some highlights on the parts of the limbs to portray/establish its angle.

With the pencil/charcoal stains on the smudge stick you previously used, apply some gray blots/irregular dots on the far sides of the abdomen. Simply dapple these areas with fairly light stippling hand strokes.

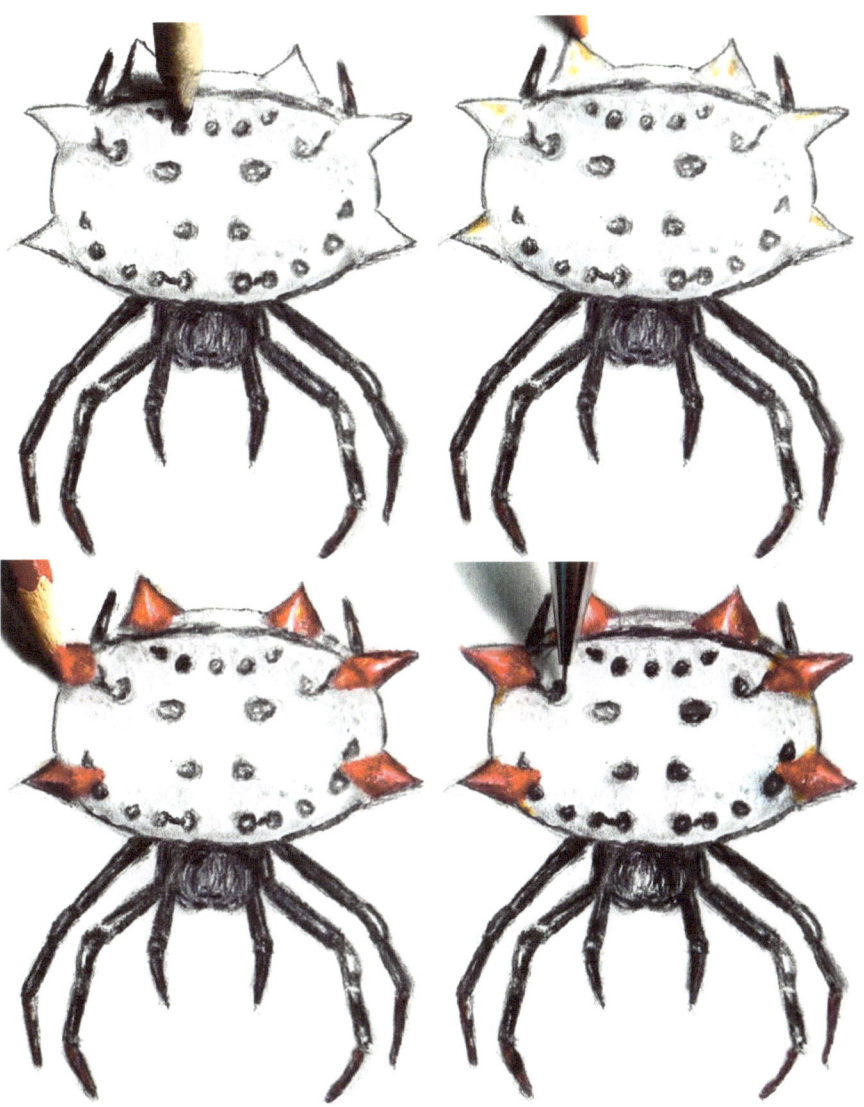

- Color the spines.

Start applying the red color tone of the spines. The red tone contains a faint orange value. To obtain this hue, apply some orange color on one side of the spines, and then overlap it with red. Leave a highlight at the center of each spine to portray its conical shape. And then apply few more orange tones around each spines.

- Make the final retouches.

Re-outline the shape of the spider especially the smudged outlines of the limbs. Re-darken the areas that should appear darker (the black spot should have the darkest tone), then cast a shadow to finalize the drawing.

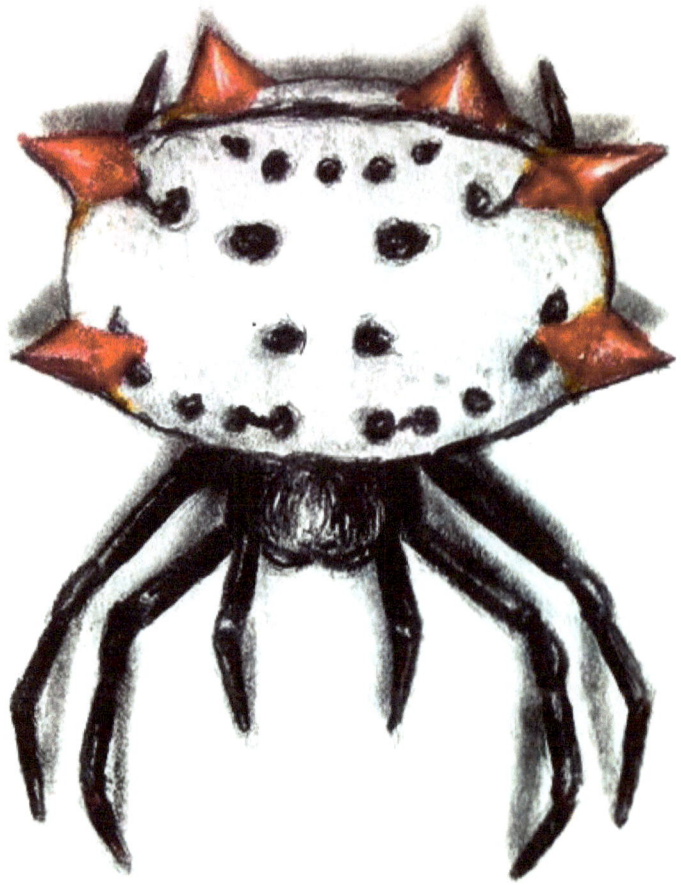

The scientific name 'gasteracantha cancriformis' is a combination of four Greek terms, 'gaster' means belly and 'acantha' means thorn, 'cancrim' was taken from the word 'cancer' which means crab, and formis means 'form'. This orbweaver can be found on shady areas of the woods (mostly on trees or around it) and at gardens covered in shrubs. The size of a female is approximately ten to thirteen millimeters in width, with a length of approximately five to nine millimeters. A male gasteracantha cancriformis is significantly smaller, with a shape having a longer length and a shorter width.

Spined Micrathena

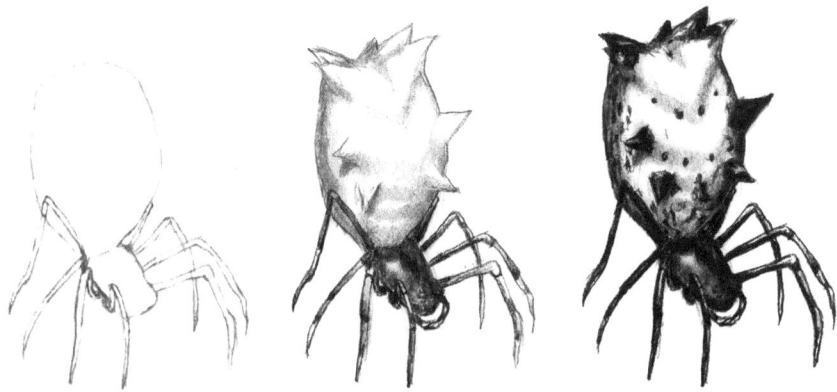

A spined micrathena spider, also called as the micrathena gracilis, is a spiky spider that is often seen in the woods, mostly on shaded areas where their prey usually reside. It belongs to the family of orb-weavers (its relatives are easily distinguished through their certain similarities, possessing some resemblance in features and choice of habitat). The spined micrathena has significantly large ophistosoma (abdomen). The abdomen contains few short spikes that usually have a different color from the surface of the abdomen.

Spined micrathena spiders are basically dark-colored (excluding the abdomen). The upper body and the limbs are black, with faint color of deep brown or a dark pitch of copper tone, which is mostly visible on the tips of the limbs (in a closer look, you might see a stripe of black and faint copper/brown color on its legs). The uniquely formed opisthosoma (abdomen) is shaped like a bean, slightly angled diagonally. The base of the abdomen is usually dirty white in color (sometimes, with random patches of black), having ten protruding short black spikes on the dorsal side that are arranged in five pairs (but male micrathena spiders have fewer spikes/spines). The sides of the abdomen have ridges, and right below the opisthosoma (underside) is a protruding portion (significantly thicker than the spines) with a blunt tip.

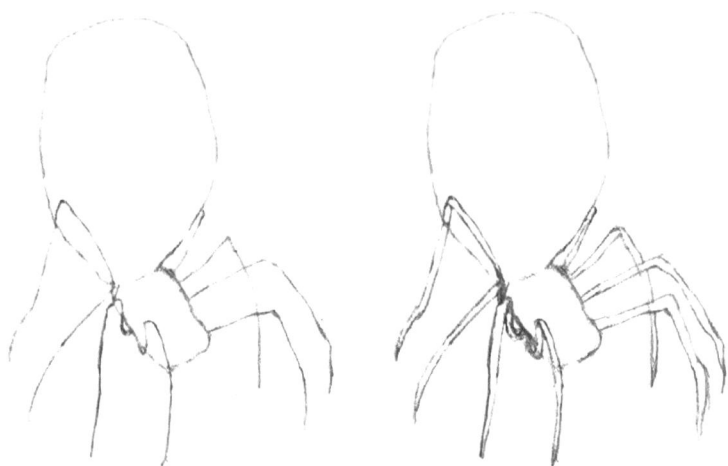

- Establish the shape of the spider.'

The large abdomen of the spined micrathena is basically oval that has atleast two times the mass of the upper body, and the upper body has a shape of an irregular oval. Establish the position/angle of the spider and use simple lines to convey the length of each limb.

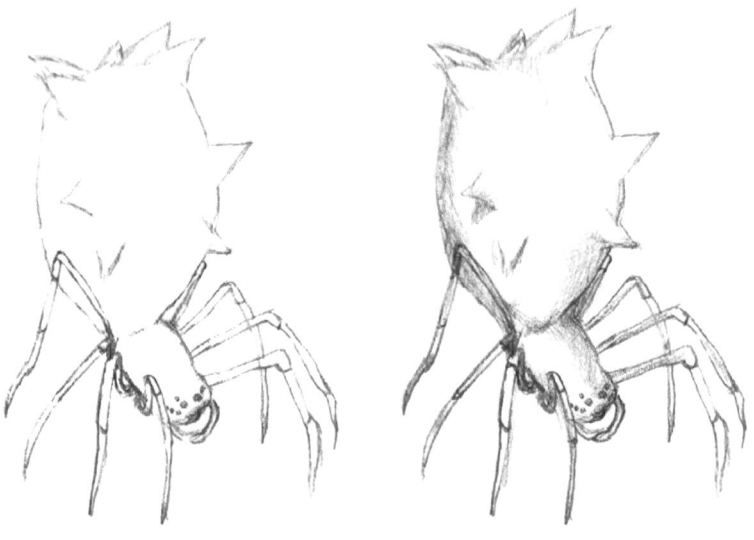

Once the basic shape of the body is defined, and the length and folds of the limbs are established, complete the primary outline of the spider by adding the thickness of the legs and the spines of the abdomen. The spines should be set in pairs, all protruding outwards from the near-edge of the abdomen; with two pairs on the lower area and others surrounding the top.

- Convey the dimensions.

Apply some faint linear shading to establish the contour shape/dimensions. Shade the farther areas of the upper body and of the abdomen. Based on the spider's position, the lower area of the abdomen and its semi-flat top (due to the spines) should appear darker, so as the farther plane (left side) of its oval-shaped structure, making the upper-center the brightest area. And for the upper body, simply put some shading on the farther portion including the farther limbs.

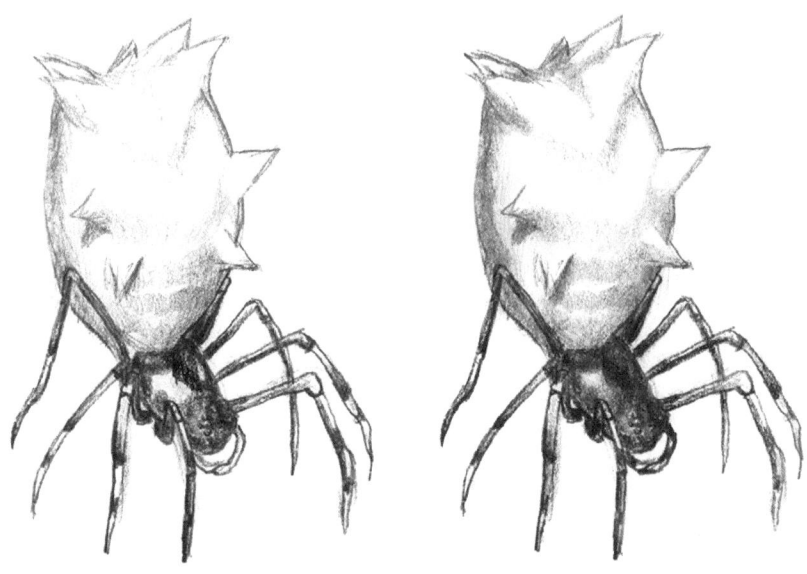

- Thicken the shading.

Elaborate the gradation. The upper body of the spined micrathena is dark-toned and the surface of the abdomen has some slopes. Thicken the shading on the upper body using fairly-heavy scribbling strokes but take note of the portions that should have a brighter value. Darken the far edges of the limbs to convey their cylindrical shapes. The farther portions of each leg should appear darker, especially the foreshortened ones (femur segments of the nearer legs).

The slopes of the abdomen reside on the levels of the spines. Only apply a faint shade because the abdomen is basically white. Use thin and light diagonal hatches, and curve them according to the surface's dimensional shape.

- Smear the shading.

Carefully smudge the shades to diminish the line marks and create a smooth toning. Then re-darken the darkest portions with another layer of shading once more.

- Add the details of the abdomen.

Once the gradation/shade value of the abdomen is properly established, add the details such as the few small dark spots rowed in two arcs (usually 2 rows having four dots). The spines are black, and the abdomen has some subtle irregular black patches mostly on the lower area and on the sides.

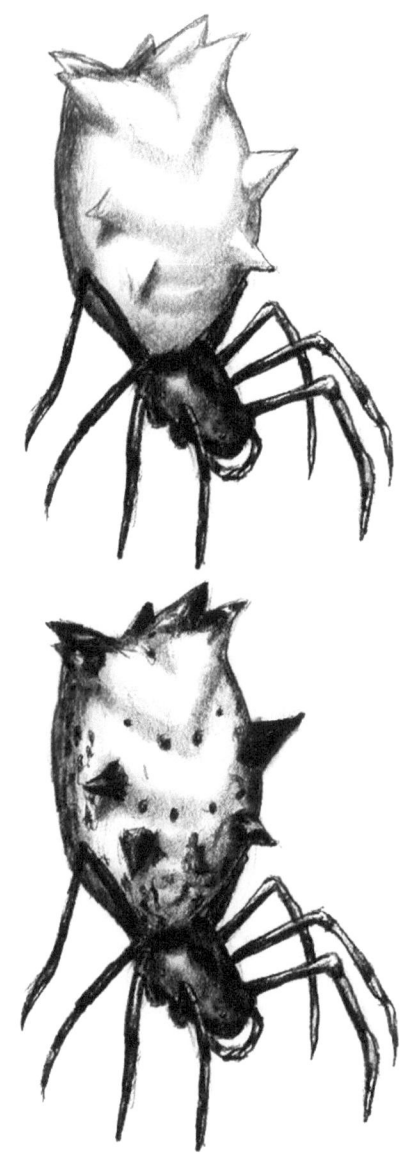

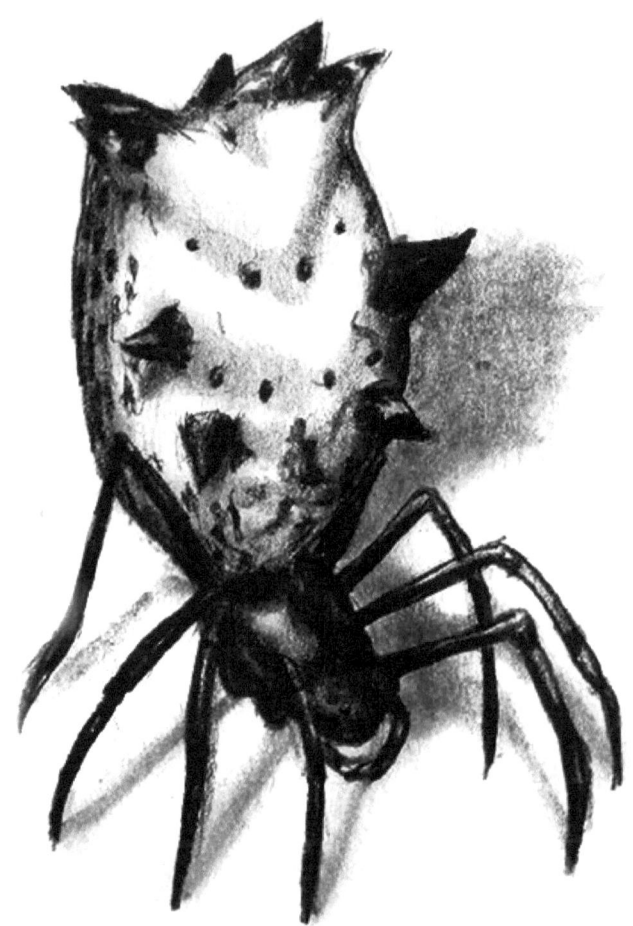

You probably won't notice the beauty of this common spider because of its size. Although, it is easy to know if the area is inhabited by this spider (or any of its related spider species) because of the orb-like formation of the webs it constructs. The disk-shaped webs are usually 3 to 7 feet from the ground, which are at least seven and up to eleven inches big, making the webs are quite noticeable. This small spider can only grow from eight to ten millimeter in size, and the males are half of the size of females (from 4 to 5 millimeter) with smaller abdomen and fewer spikes. Male spined micrathenas are lighter in color and do not construct disk-shaped webs; instead, they only use their webs for mating purposes when they are mature enough.

Red-knee Tarantula

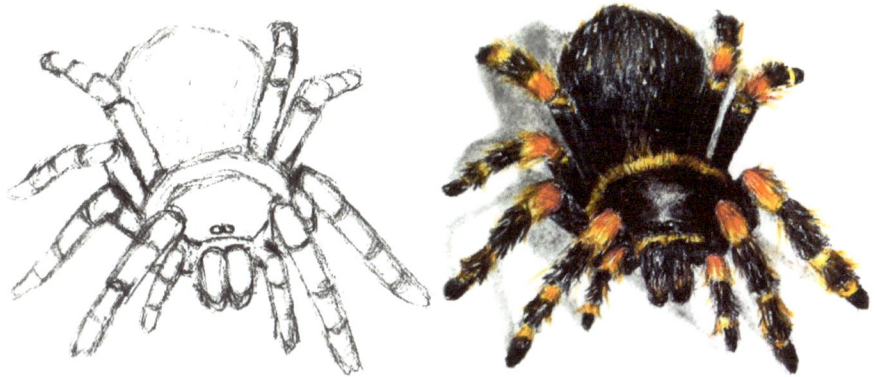

The red knee tarantula is one of the most preferred type of tarantula genus by arachnid enthusiasts and spider breeders because of its docile nature. It can also be handled by those who are just starting to keep arachnid species as pets due to its relatively calm nature. This burrower (like most tarantulas) will often stay on its burrow most of the time, and patiently wait for its prey (and avoid any potential threat). If disturbed or mishandled, it will only attack by using uricating hairs (by flicking its leg) instead of biting, and the venom level it releases is low and not life-threatening to humans (but for safety measures, you should still ask for a proper medical attention, especially if you received more than one bite). The red knee tarantula, also known as brachypelma smithi, is common in Mexico, specifically, to the western side of Sierra Madre (Occidental and del Sur) mountain, having a body size of approximately four inches, the leg length could grow long for approximately six inches. The size of the male and female is relatively the same, the only difference is the body proportion (males have smaller bodies but have longer limbs).

This tarantula is bicolored with strong color values. Its shape is common for tarantula species (round semi-flat upper body and bulky oval abdomen). The color is a combination of black and orange/red. The upper body (cephalothorax) with a dull black tone thickly margined with orange. The abdomen is black, containing few strands of pale orange. Its limbs have stripes of black and orange, with the folding joints/ knees having the orange color of the strongest value. The femur is always black, and the section of patella/knees is reddish orange. The alternating colors are continued (stripes) down to the tip (tarsus), and this color rendition is uniform to red knee tarantulas. The color value of the orange segments (as well as its thickness) diminishes as it reaches the tip of the limb.

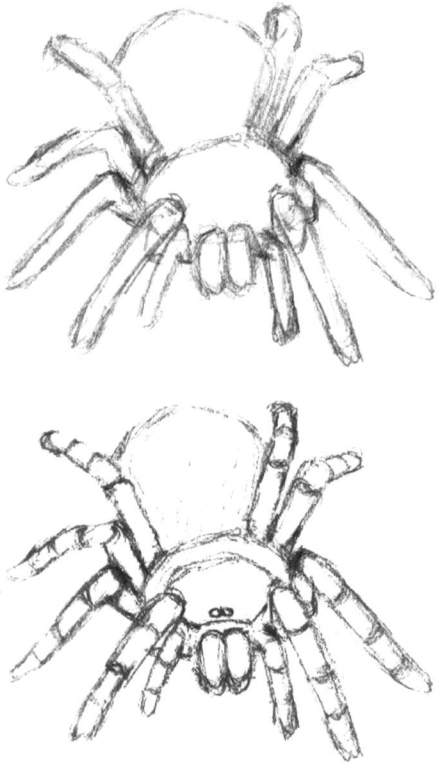

- Sketch the basic outline of the spider.

Sketch the complete shape of the spider including the parts that would not be seen due to the viewpoint. The thickness of the abdomen becomes more apparent when the spider is viewed on a higher angle, and the upper body would seem flat. The actual length of the body is affected because the shapes are foreshortened.

Establish how the limbs are folded. Draw each of them as a whole to easily distinguish its proper length, including the portions overlapped by the ones at the front. Some portions/segments of the forelimbs should also be foreshortened.

- Erase the unnecessary line marks and add the details.

Clean up the drawing once the outline of the shape is recognized. Erase the portions that would not be seen on this view angle, and then add the other lining details necessary; the stripes on the legs, the dorsal eyes, and the outlining inside the carapace. Make some short contour lines on the abdomen to guide you how the abdominal hairs should be established.

- Apply the shade value of the abdomen.

Begin establishing the gradation of the body by starting with the abdomen. Use fairly thick line strokes; gradually fill up the area with vertical hatches but leave some highlights to convey its hairy texture.

Smudge the shading with light hand strokes. Use short strokes (follow the vertical pattern of the line layers). Then after smudging the previous shading, apply another layer of shade on the parts that should appear darker. Darken the sides and the lower area of the abdomen to convey its spherical shape.

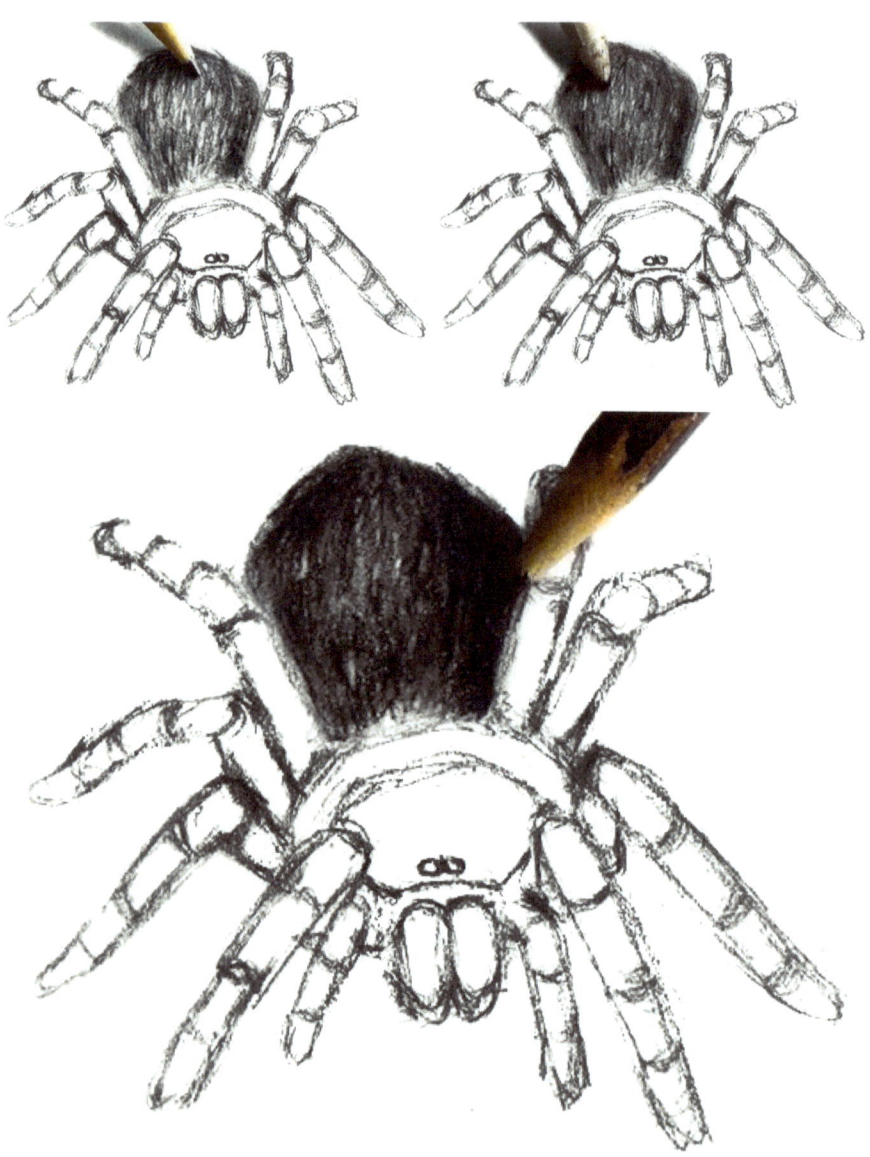

- Put some white and orange line marks on the abdomen.

Apply some short lines of orange to the upper portion of the abdomen. And also put some short white lines to create some highlights. Use thin lines with fairly heavy hand strokes.

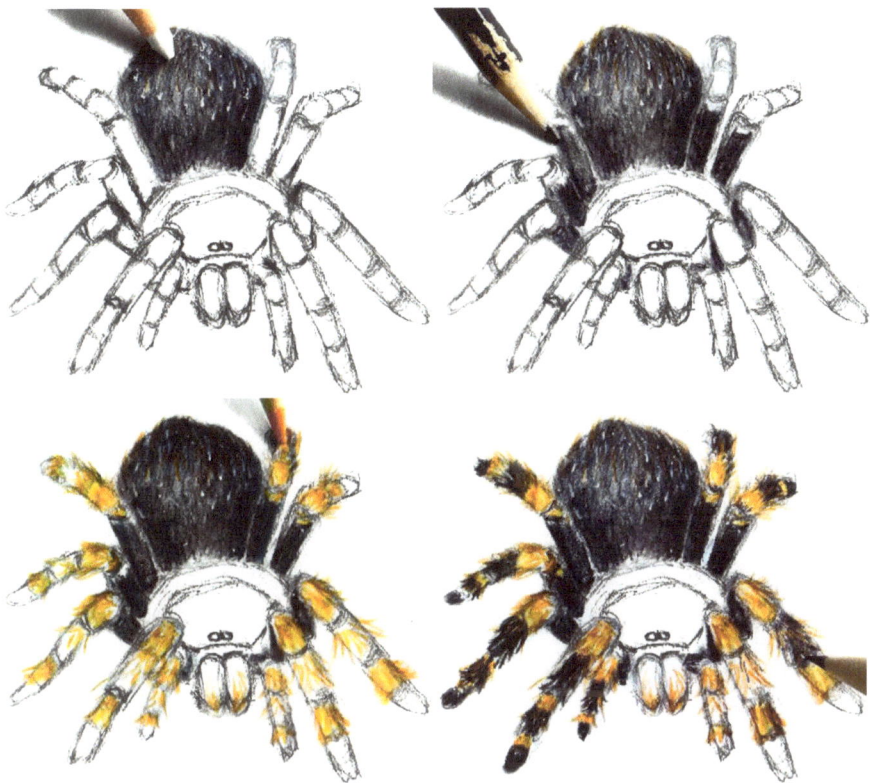

- Shade the dark areas of the legs.

The femur segments of the limbs are black. Simply apply a thick shading on this portion. The sides of the limbs and the lower area (connected to the base) should be darker than the middle area of the femur segments.

- Apply the color of the limbs.

The limbs contain a stripe pattern of orange and black. The thickness of the stripes become thinner as it reaches the tip of the leg. The color sequence starts with black (this was previously applied) then orange; the femur is black, and the patella is orange, and so on. The limbs have five stripes in total.

Apply some short line strokes of orange spiking out of the outline to all the segments of the limbs, but the segments that should be orange must contain more orange strands. Use different line weight and line thickness. The strands should spike downwards from its base, but if the limb segment is pointing upward then the hair strand should also spike upward. The black sections should also contain few orange hairs.

- Darken the dark sections of the limbs.

Apply short spiking lines of black and overlap the orange lines with black, but only the sections that should be black.

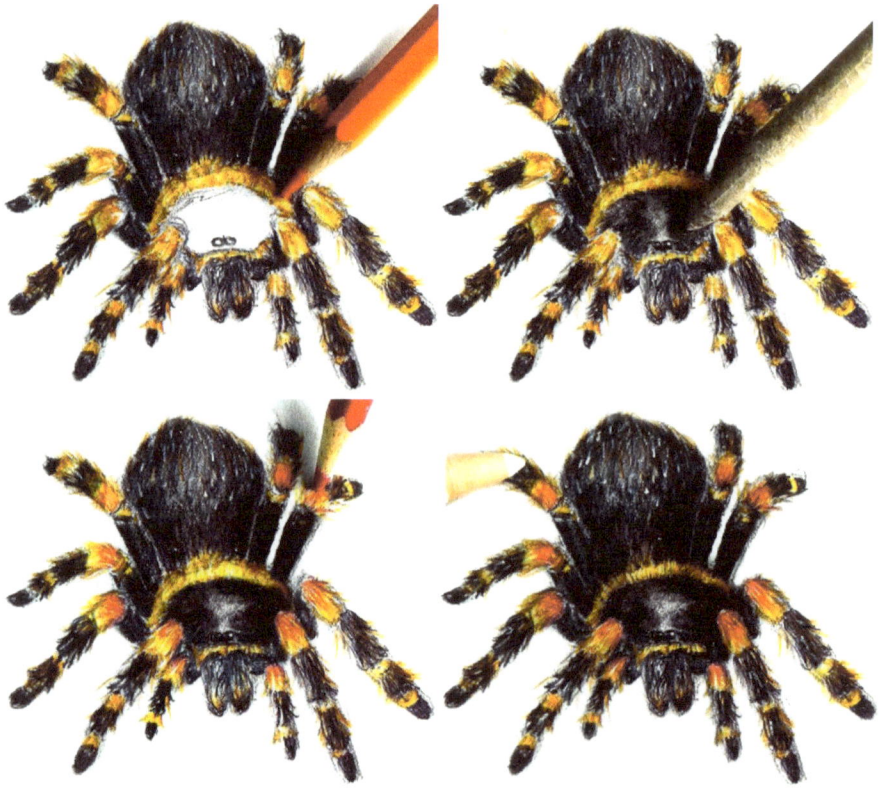

- Finish the carapace.

The carapace is margined with thick orange. Fill up this portion with hatches of orange line strokes. Then shade the middle section. Smear the shaded area, and then apply another shade on the sides of the carapace's slope to make the center appear brighter.

- Apply some red strands on the knees.

Put some short strokes of red strands on the segment of patella (knees of the spider) to create a stronger and darker value of orange (this is why they are called red knee tarantulas). Simply follow the pattern of the previous strands and spike the short red lines out of the base/main outline.

- Finalize the drawing.

Re-darken the darkest portions of the spider. Darken the exposed sections of the limbs that are overlapped by the other. Re-darken the sides of the carapace and the foreshortened areas of the forelimbs. Apply some few thin line strokes on the orange section of the carapace to convey its hairy surface. Add some few more highlights to the limbs then cast a shadow.

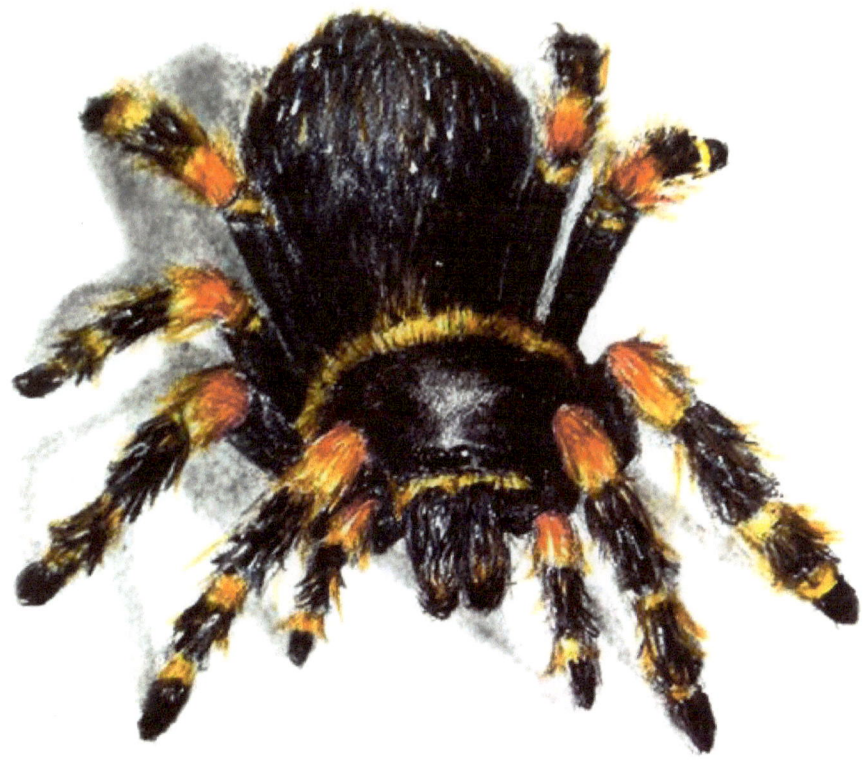

Ladybird Spider

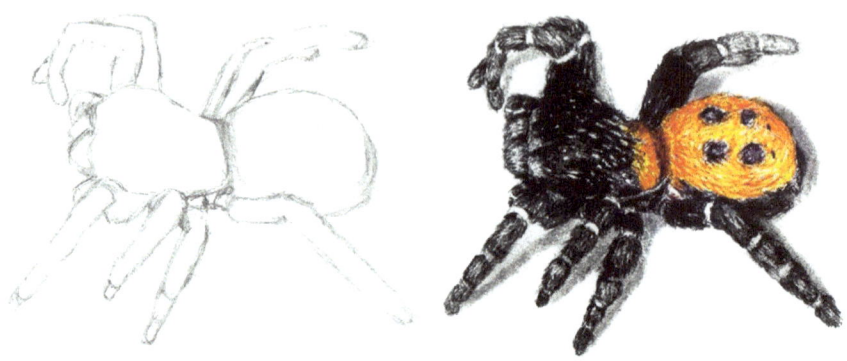

Ladybird spiders are small black spiders with some observable coloring and abdominal print features. They can be seen mostly on dry habitats, inside small and shallow underground tubes. Males are also seen on surface when they are in search for their mates, and they would live on a found shelter where they mates reside. Ladybird spiders are often discovered living not far from one another. They belong to the spider family of eresidae, and categorized into different subspecies with few noticeable differences. Females can grow a bit larger than the males (nearly an inch).

A ladybird spider contains a vibrant red to deep orange color on its abdomen, with four black dots at the center (dorsal view), hence, the name 'ladybird spider'. It has white stripes on its limbs and few short white hairs, contrasting the general black body. In some cases, the strong red value of the opisthosoma (abdominal area) is partially spread on the area of its thorax and hind legs (third and fourth pair of legs). The body shape of a lady bird spider is basically formed by two fairly round bases, with semi-flat sloping surfaces. The size of its lower body (opisthosoma) is nearly the same size as the upper body including the head (prosoma). Its limbs are fairly thick with blunt-point tips (tarsus). In most cases, the deep black tone of its body gradually fades as it reaches the tips of its limbs, so as the red value (if present) of its hind legs (creating small and faint yellow marks along the white stripes of the legs).

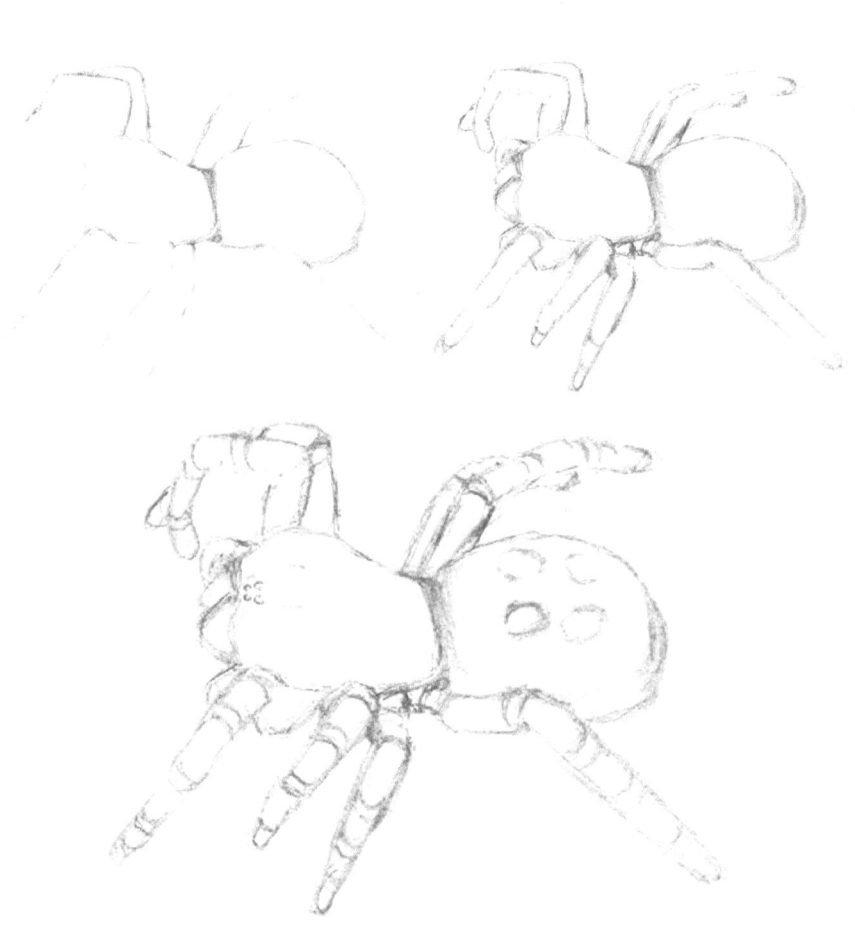

- Establish the Position and shape of the spider.

Draw a semi-disk shaped oval for the abdomen, and an irregularly shaped oval for the upper body. In this angle (side of mid-aerial view), the side connecting to the abdomen should be flat, and the upper area should be protruding (the area of the head).

Establish the length of the legs with singular lines, in this way, it is easier to convey how it curves and fold. Take note of the view angle the spider is positioned.

- Define the legs.

Establish the proportion of the legs properly. Define the outline dimensions of each leg according to their angles. Due to the spider's viewpoint, some portions of the limbs need to be foreshortened. The nearer legs are folded in a manner which their true lengths are not shown. The length and shape of the femur segments should be modified. The femur segment of the second leg is completely hidden, while the others only show a small portion of it since this segment is pointed forward towards the viewpoint.

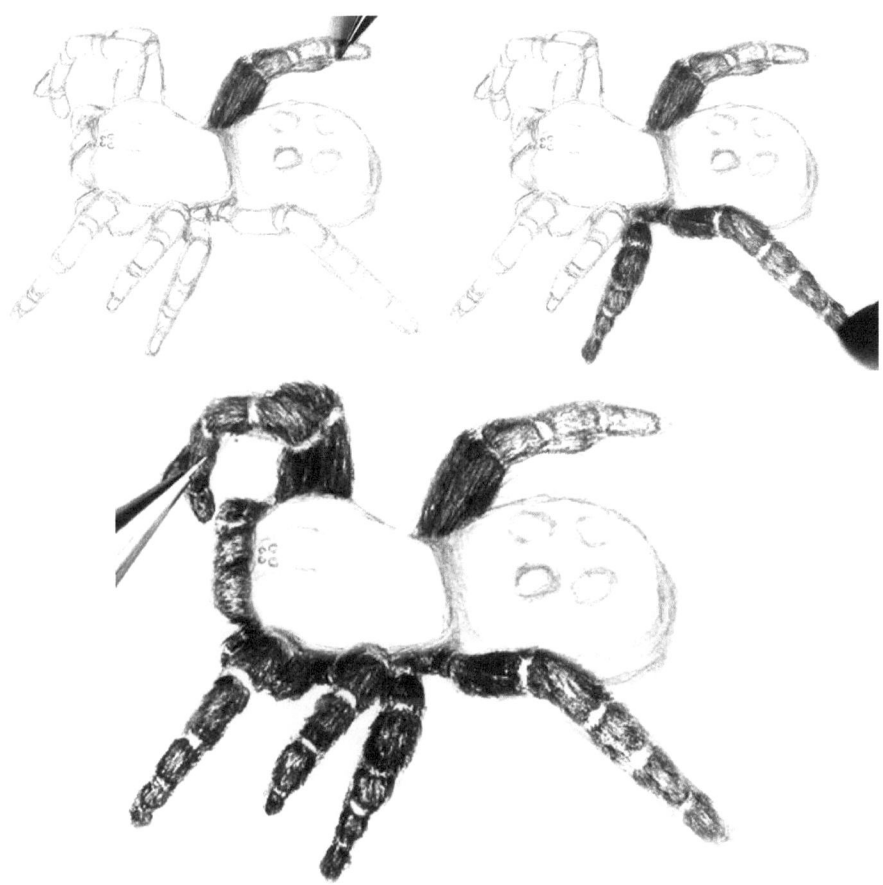

- Place the details.

Once the shape of the spider is defined, draw the details of its body. The unique feature of the ladybird's spider is its four black spots on its abdomen; use reference lines to properly lay out the four black spots. Draw the bars of stripes on the limbs. There are four horizontal white stripes on each limb, it begins above the knees/patella, and three more on the way down. These stripes would help depict the mass and cylindrical shape of the legs.

- Convey the texture and shade of the limbs.

The legs are covered in fairly thick black fur, paling down as it reaches the tip/tarsus. The furs are sectioned between each stripe, as if the stripes are bandages around the furry coating.

Adjust the pressure on your line strokes depending on the section of the limb. Use dark and fairly thick lines on the inner areas and thin lines on the far edges of the leg segments near the base/body. Gradually adjust the pitch/darkness as you get to the tip.

The pedipalps and its thick chelicerae contain the same furry texture as the legs' with the palps having two white stripes each.

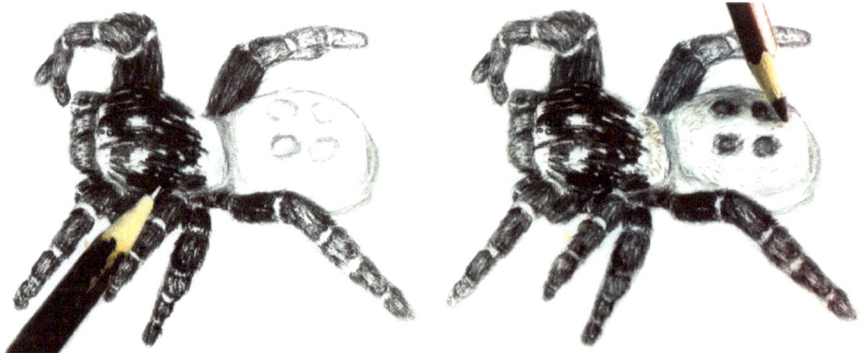

- Shade the upper body of the spider.

The carapace is generally black, with few thick white short hairs contrasting its surface. Shade the entire area with thick line strokes while leaving subtle highlights.

Shade the side of the abdomen which should also be black, using the same short and thin line strokes. Fill up the area with subtle changes in shade value according to the portion (farther sides having darker shade value).

- Start coloring the abdomen.

The fur of the abdomen is basically reddish-orange. To obtain this color value and texture, use three different colors that could effectively portray a darker tone of orange. Take note of the small portion of the upper body that also has this color value.

To effectively depict the texture, fill up the area with thin and short lines with multiple layers of different color. Use light brown, orange and red.

Use brown as a darker tone of the orange color. Make some few short lines with light hand strokes around the contour shape of the abdomen.

Fill up the area with orange short lines. Keep on following the contour shape of the surface and fill it with short lines having different thickness/thinness and line weight (pressure on hand strokes).

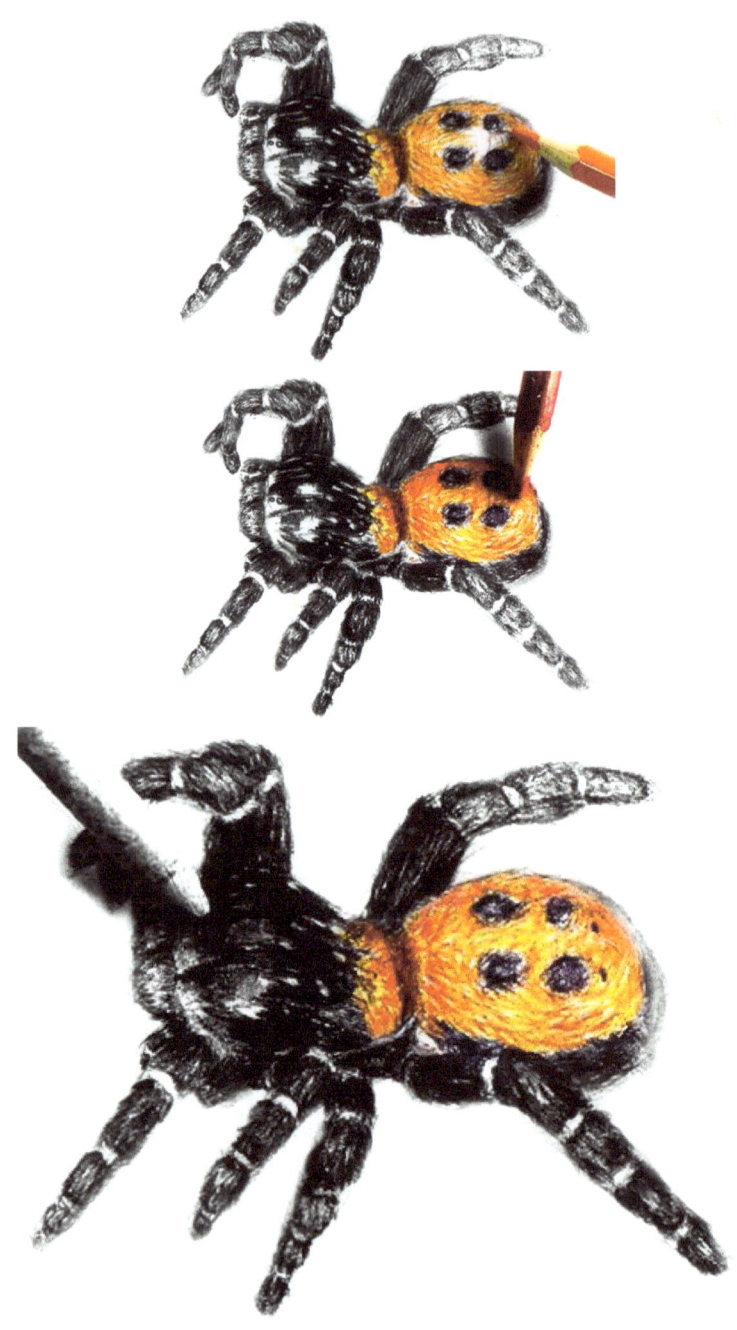

Finally, make some few short lines for the darkest orange value using red color.

- Evenly smear the shade with a smudge stick (or with anything, you prefer). The shade on the robust area should be a little lighter compared to the downward slope near the abdomen. You should also darken the farther areas of the carapace to depict its dimension values according to the point of view

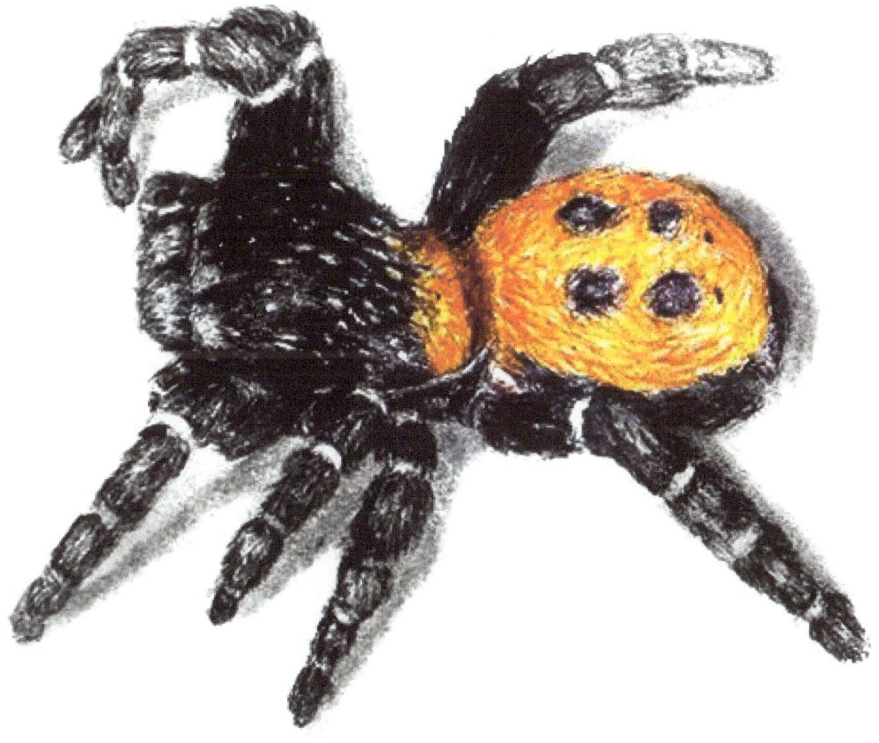

Thank you for reading.

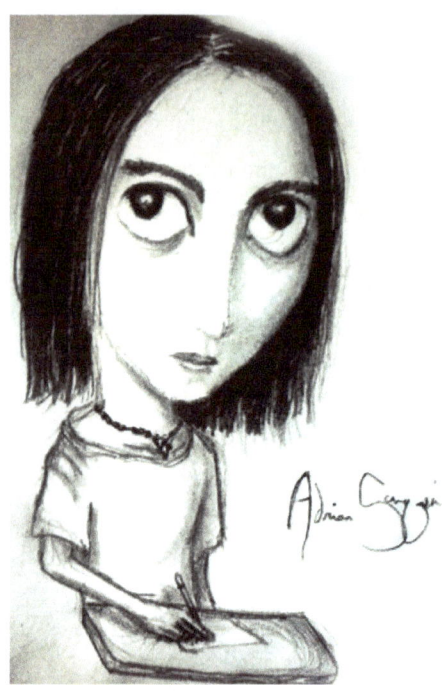

Author Bio

Check out some of my other books:

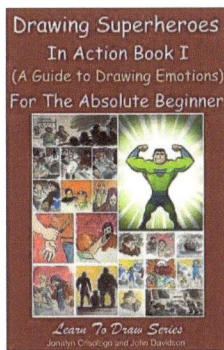

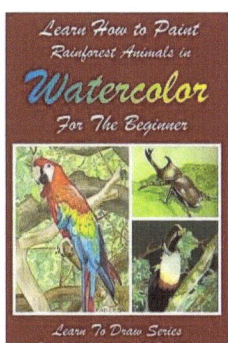

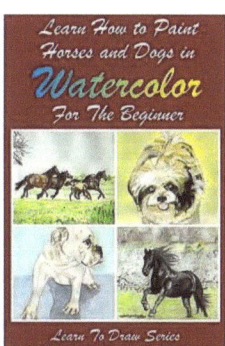

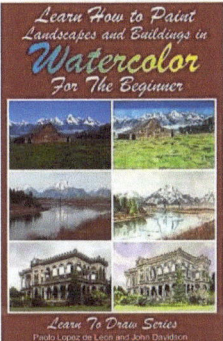

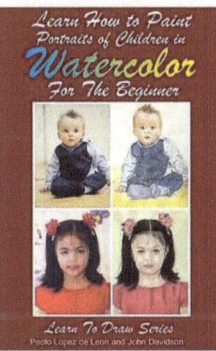

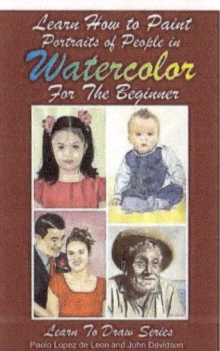

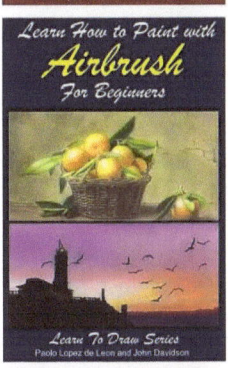

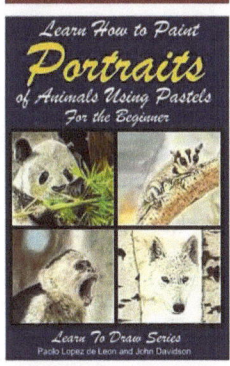

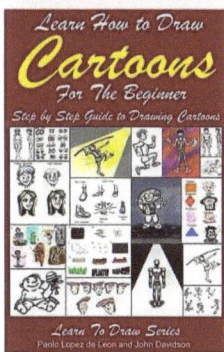

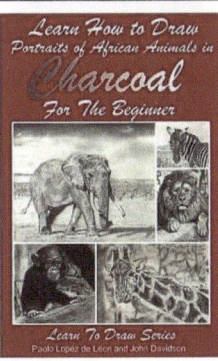

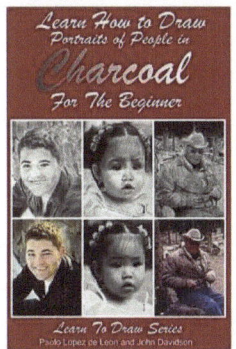

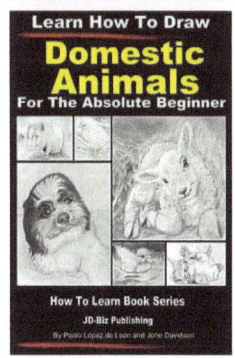

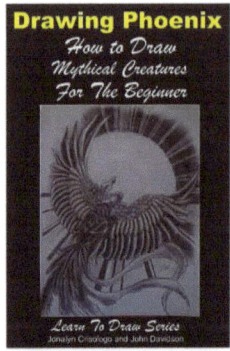

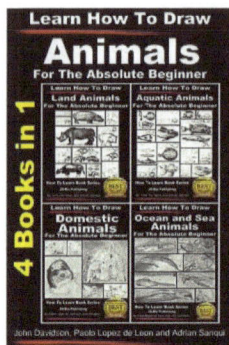

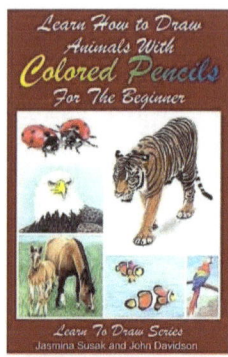

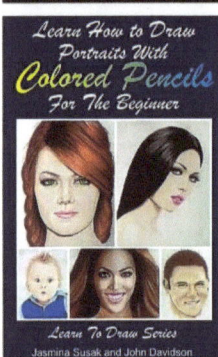

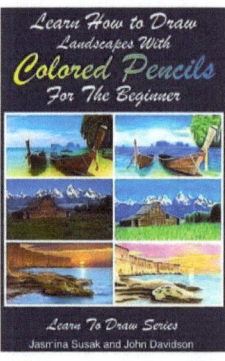

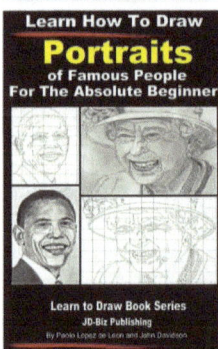

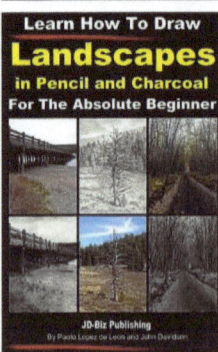

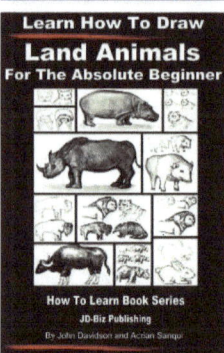

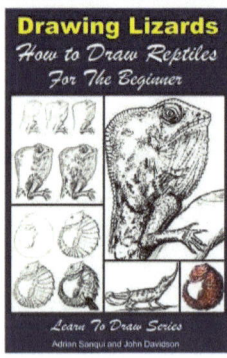

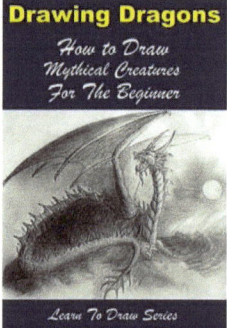

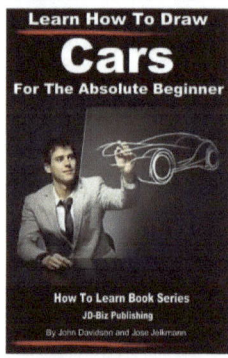

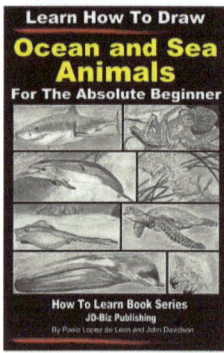

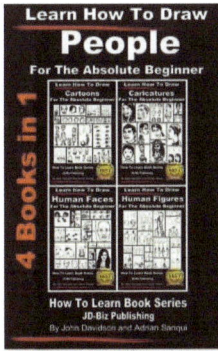

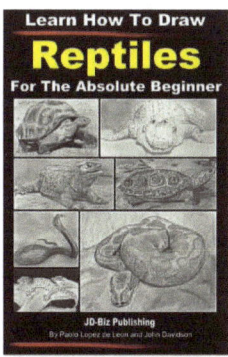

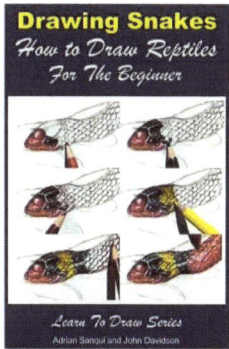

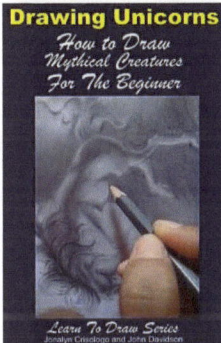

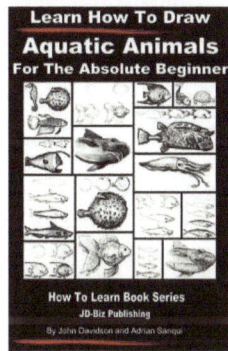

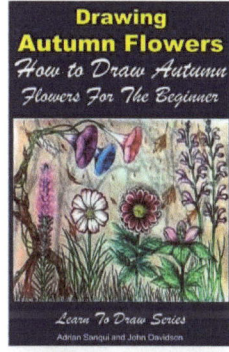

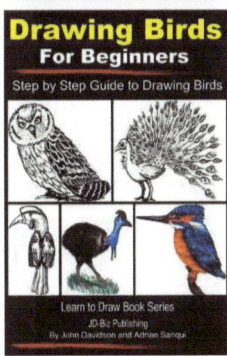

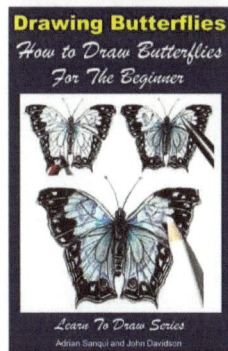

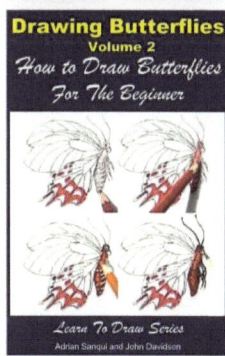

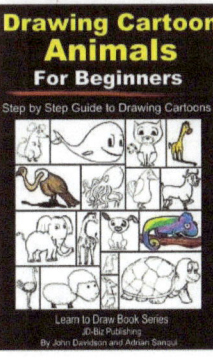

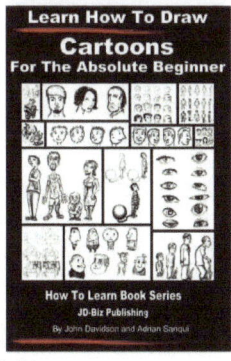

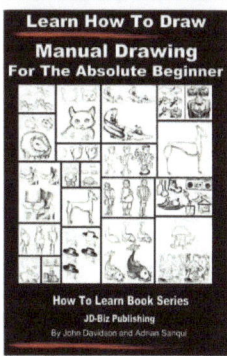

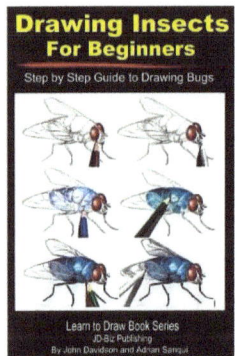

Drawing Insects For Beginners
Step by Step Guide to Drawing Bugs
Learn to Draw Book Series
JD-Biz Publishing
By John Davidson and Adrian Sanqui

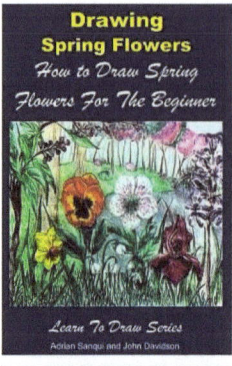

Drawing Spring Flowers
How to Draw Spring Flowers For The Beginner
Learn To Draw Series
Adrian Sanqui and John Davidson

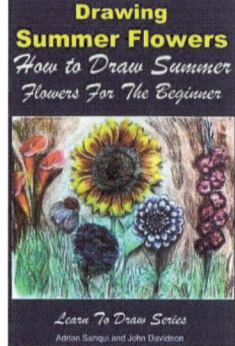

Drawing Summer Flowers
How to Draw Summer Flowers For The Beginner
Learn To Draw Series
Adrian Sanqui and John Davidson

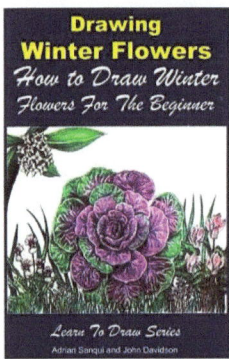

Drawing Winter Flowers
How to Draw Winter Flowers For The Beginner
Learn To Draw Series
Adrian Sanqui and John Davidson

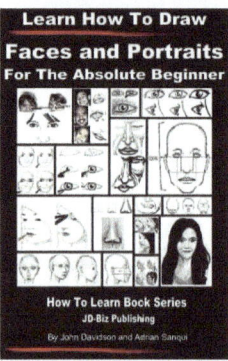

Learn How To Draw Faces and Portraits For The Absolute Beginner
How To Learn Book Series
JD-Biz Publishing
By John Davidson and Adrian Sanqui

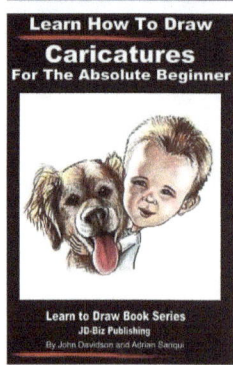

Learn How To Draw Caricatures For The Absolute Beginner
Learn to Draw Book Series
JD-Biz Publishing
By John Davidson and Adrian Sanqui

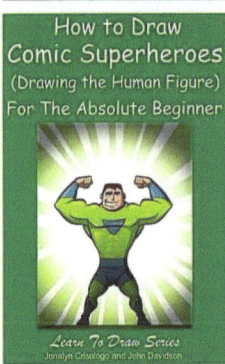

How to Draw Comic Superheroes
(Drawing the Human Figure) For The Absolute Beginner
Learn To Draw Series
Jonalyn Crisologo and John Davidson

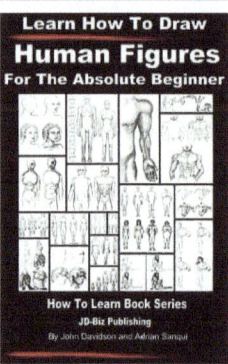

Learn How To Draw Human Figures For The Absolute Beginner
How To Learn Book Series
JD-Biz Publishing
By John Davidson and Adrian Sanqui

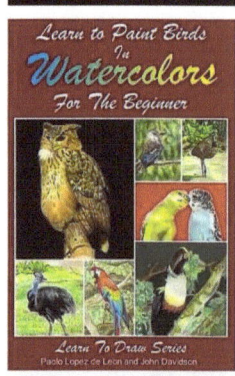

Learn to Paint Birds In Watercolors For The Beginner
Learn To Draw Series
Paolo Lopez de Leon and John Davidson

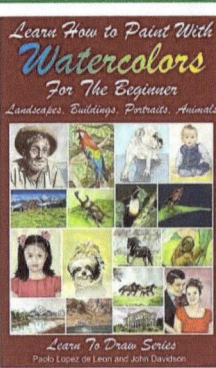

Learn How to Paint With Watercolors For The Beginner
Landscapes, Buildings, Portraits, Animals
Learn To Draw Series
Paolo Lopez de Leon and John Davidson

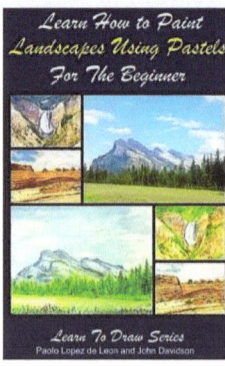

Learn How to Paint Landscapes Using Pastels For The Beginner
Learn To Draw Series
Paolo Lopez de Leon and John Davidson

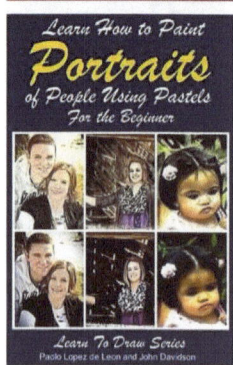

Learn How to Paint Portraits of People Using Pastels For the Beginner
Learn To Draw Series
Paolo Lopez de Leon and John Davidson

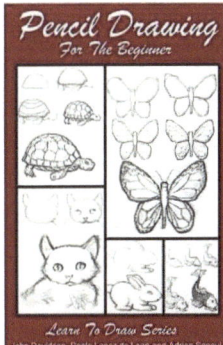

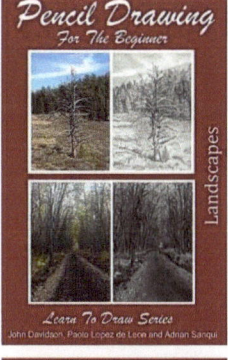

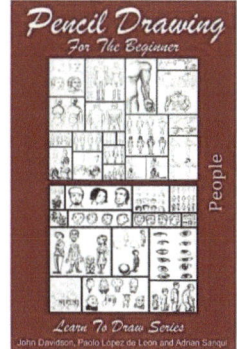

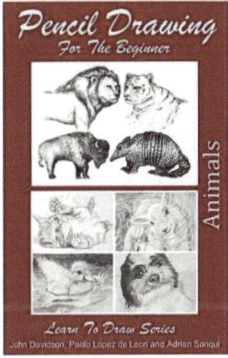

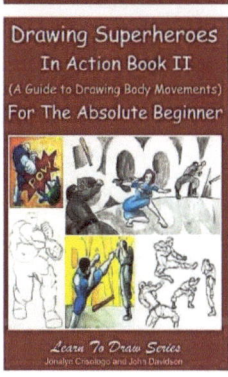

Publisher

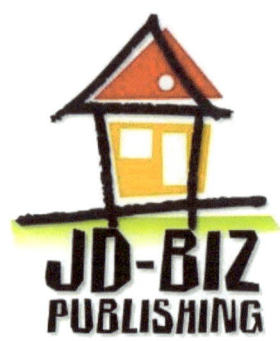

JD-Biz Corp

P O Box 374

Mendon, Utah 84325

http://www.jd-biz.com/

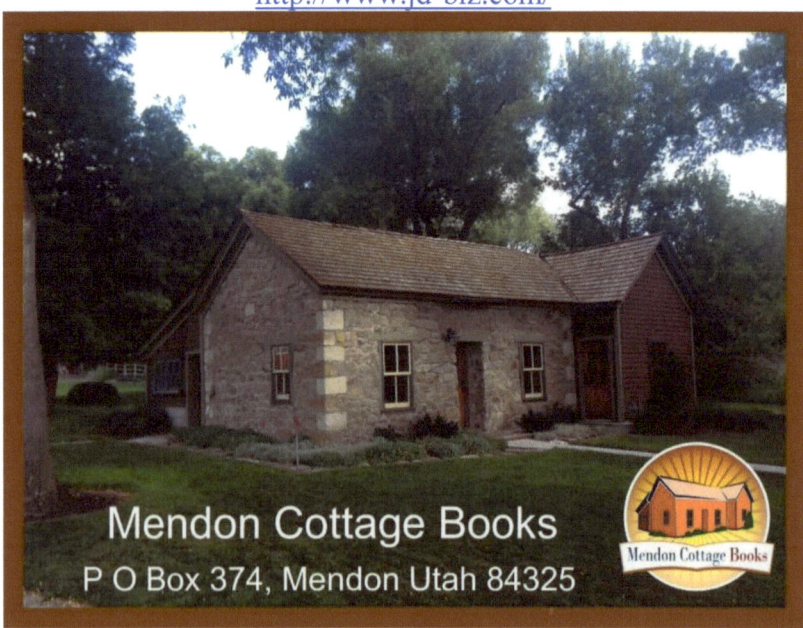